AMAZING
NEARNESS

Father Tadeusz Dajczer

A M A Z I N G
NEARNESS

Meditations on the Eucharist

PARACLETE PRESS
BREWSTER, MASSACHUSETTS

Amazing Nearness: Meditations on the Eucharist

2012 First Printing

Copyright 2009 by Bolesław Szewc

ISBN 978-1-61261-200-3

Original Title: *Zdumiewająca bliskość*
Translated by Rev. Bryan Storey with edits for this Paraclete Press edition,
first published in 2009. Published in co-edition with Eucharistic Renewal
Books, 1 Chy an Pronter, Bossiney Road, Tintagel, Cornwall, PL34 0AQ,
UK, Phone/fax +44 1 840 770663, e-mail: books@eucharisticrenewal.org,
website: eucharisticrenewal.org.

Nihil obstat
Rev. Thomas M. Kocik
Censor Deputatus

Imprimatur
+Most Reverend George W. Coleman, D.D., S.T.L.
Bishop of Fall River, Massachusetts
February 6, 2012

*The nihil obstat and imprimatur are official declarations that a book or
pamphlet is free from doctrinal or moral error. No implication is contained
therein that those who grant the nihil obstat or imprimatur agree with the
contents or statements expressed.*

Scripture quotations are taken from the *Revised Standard Version of the Bible*,
Catholic Edition, © 1965 and 1966 by the Division of Christian Education of
the National Council of the Churches of Christ in the USA, and are used by
permission.

Library of Congress Cataloging-in-Publication Data

Dajczer, Tadeusz.
  [Zdumiewajaca bliskosc. English]
  Amazing nearness : meditations on the Eucharist / Tadeusz Dajczer.
    p. cm.
  ISBN 978-1-61261-200-3 (hc jacket)
  1. Lord's Supper—Catholic Church—Meditations. 2. Spirituality—Catholic
Church—Meditations. I. Title.
  BX2169.D3313 2012
  234'.163—dc23   2012003951

10 9 8 7 6 5 4 3 2 1

Published in North America in 2012 by Paraclete Press
Brewster, Massachusetts
www.paracletepress.com
Printed in the United States of America

CONTENTS

FOREWORD

BY

Archbishop Joseph Michalik

METROPOLITAN OF PRAEMISLIA AND
CHAIRMAN OF THE POLISH CONFERENCE
OF BISHOPS

L ove is a special gift; it is born in the heart; it embraces the whole man. Yet more, it penetrates one who is loved. It forgets hardship, sacrifice, suffering; it bears all things and never ends (1 Cor. 13:7–8); it gives meaning to and uniquely motivates our lives. It fears nothing; it inspires our goals; amazingly, it can realize them. That is how it is with human love; with God's love, it is much more. St. John sums up: God is Love.

Yet we have to talk about Love, especially as there is so much to say. I suspect that the author of *Amazing Nearness* is unable not to talk about this Love. We are curious to know how he experiences It. We want to know what he is going to tell us. He experiences It as the amazing nearness of God's Love in the Holy Eucharist; he strengthens us by saying that in seeking Him we are already finding Him.

The experienced mountaineering guide knows that climbing requires instructions and warnings; he shares his knowledge.

On the way to God we need silence, much quieting of imagination, desires, emotions, avoiding unnecessary words, the need to simplify everything, interior poverty, a purifying emptiness that can only be filled by infinite Love. This *love is not found through knowledge* but through contact with and nearness to the Eucharist.

Man only sees what he wants to see, the author warns; we may not notice that God loves us in an exceptional way, that He is moved in the face of man's misfortunes and pains, that He sympathizes with him in every daily event. Yet compassion is not enough; we need God Himself. We find Him in the Holy Eucharist.

This book is an exceptional commentary on Pope Benedict XVI's encyclical *Deus Caritas Est*. It explains and helps us understand love as *agape* and *eros* in our relationship with the Eucharist. Indeed, it is exactly here that we experience the affinity, communion, and mutual love that can transform us into This One who has first loved us.

This book offers beautiful, praying theology. It inspires by revealing authentic experiences. It is a rapid current of dialogue revealing new pearls of living faith.

This experienced, caring author also warns us of the power of Hatred; it is not to be disregarded. It shows that *the final goal of my interior life is not sanctification in itself but my complete dedication to the Church* because Christ lives here; here we serve others; here we receive the gift of the Eucharist, which sustains us on the way, uniting the soul with God.

The book faces difficult questions; looking for answers, it praises God's untiring love. He is close to man. He is actually in love with man. Our tragedy is that so often we do not discover, appreciate, or effectively benefit from this for our ongoing development.

The Reverend Professor also wants to help draw the response from us that pines for Infinity. So he leads us to humility in recognizing that we are far away from these extraordinary discoveries. We only sense this with faith and touch it with weak love. Yet we achieve much if we notice the value of and need for this *way of heart* in the pathways that long for God.

We thank the author for his warm optimism, for his faith in man that each of us can be better, can even be a saint; it suffices to discover Love as: *God has a liking for men of violence, for these mad ones who conquer the Kingdom of Heaven (cf. Mt. 11:12). They conquer not being worthy of this Kingdom. God does not call the decent to sanctity but sinners.* We have a great need for this message; it is about everything that is really important. Let us help one another on this extraordinary road by prayer with Jesus in the Most Holy Eucharist.

+ Joseph Michalik

AMAZING
NEARNESS

Part I

He Seeks Until
He is Weary

In my daily life, I am constantly getting lost. Yet that means He can constantly find me. The more I need Him, the closer He is. I can ceaselessly discover that *in weariness He sought me.*[1] This means loving until weary. Because of Original Sin He constantly searches for us to the point of weariness and exhaustion, humanly speaking.

In the Eucharistic encounter, Jesus regularly finds me quite lost. Yet I am normally lost, needing to be found. So no need for regrets. If I am lost I can only be found in Eucharistic love. He can only find me

---

1. *Quaerens me, sedisti lassus – In weariness You sought me.* The verse coming from the sequence read in the Divine Office of the last week of the Church Year. It is a clear reference to Christ's meeting with the Samaritan woman (Jn. 4:6).

when I am lost and beginning to search for Him. Love needs two. It is a grace always given to me to seek Him through faith, hope, and love.

He never stops looking for me even though, humanly speaking, He is "wearily exhausted." This search leads Him to the Cross. There is no defeat or end there; the Cross converts into the powerful glory of the Resurrection. That is my loving salvation. Our Eucharistic God always reveals Himself while hiding so that I can choose to reject Him.

He is wanting to find me at every moment. He can receive me; I may meet Him especially in the Eucharist, rather as Mary Magdalene met Him after the Resurrection. Rejoice that all apparent loss keeps coming back with ever-greater power. After all, if the One who had forgiven her everything died forever, then forgiveness "finished" and no longer had any meaning. If He had been defeated by the Cross, then she would have lost too. The forgiveness would be over. The wonder of discovering the sought-after Jesus restored every conceivable meaning to her daily life.

I am often quite lost at Mass. Although it seems like that with everything at times. Yet in Eucharistic love, everything comes back to me. It is like Mary Magdalene's situation. Holy Communion should really be my being receptive to His redeeming love. As Pope Benedict XVI says,[2] it is both *agape* and *eros*. In the Eucharist, God both seeks and finds me.

When I feel lost at Mass this is a redeeming opportunity. **He gives me** His Body.[3] **He is shedding** His Blood for me lost in earthly life. He restores me to closeness with Him. I will be found more and more according to the strength of my desire and hope.

In these moments of utter helplessness, He attracts me by grace because He wants me to discover His pouring out of Eucharistic love. *In every Mass You seek me out. It is You who are, not I. You are always the first to make the move. When I am lost, worrying that everything has already gone and I can't get back, You find me and say: "Look, I am here on the altar."*

He alone is looking for me. In times of crisis, when I feel alone and unwanted, I need to hold on tightly to this puzzling truth. Although I am utterly lost, He

---

2. Cf. the Encyclical Letter: *Deus caritas est*, 9-10.

3. In the original Greek version the words of consecration are used in the present tense.

is always searching for me. Finally I will find everything in Him. Everything comes from Him. In this He wants to attract me more deeply to desire Him alone. He wants me to understand that my family and friends need me nothing like He does. After all, we humans are limited in love; He is unlimited. Sooner or later I will have to discover that only God wants me for myself.

Maybe I will learn not to resent human limitations; I will let Him need others in me; others will then benefit from being sought by Him. This is the law of Love: finally to gain most of the lost souls. We need to discover what it means to be longed for by God. He seems to say: *You are not looking for me anywhere near enough. You need to fall in love with Me. You are still lacking faith.*

I don't live by faith very much. I often live as if He is not there. To live by faith is constantly to think of Him. What is He doing **now?** What is He doing when I am getting up, washing, when I am getting ready to go out? Is he resting? Is He looking? Is He far away? What is He doing when I am hurriedly having breakfast, thinking more of my job than of Him and thereby getting lost even more?

When I am hurrying to Mass only out of a sense of duty, *He is seeking me until He is worn out.*

I should be full of hope at the thought that He is always looking for me, especially as our Church keeps me so close to His redeeming Eucharistic love.

When I go to Mass He may grant me the gift of faith, and I will see Him alive just like Mary Magdalene after the Resurrection. Then I will cry out like her: *Rabbuni! Master!* Mass can be like that for me, even without words when my heart filled with faith will be happy in the conviction that He is so close.

After all, by faith I can "touch" Him. I am more privileged than Mary Magdalene on Easter morning. She had not yet touched Him. He sent her with a mission to the Apostles. As if He wanted to tell her or rather to tell me: *You will really "touch" me by faith when by the power of words I come to the Eucharistic altar completing my Redemption. It is only completed when you receive it totally in your constantly lost, anxious condition. You will be able to "touch" Me when after the Eucharistic prayer I come to you in Holy Communion.*

In this, I am more privileged than Mary Magdalene. Yet does receiving Communion bring me to be grateful? Do I hurry to tell Him: *Master! It is so good it is You. You, the Resurrected One, present in Your incomprehensibly redemptive loving concern for me. When, as I hope, You introduce me into Your glory, I will see my whole life was Your constantly searching for me in Your redeeming, Eucharistic love.*

The Gift of
Forbearance

I get so disheartened. I am frequently in touch with the Lord, yet I am always falling away from Him. I am always failing in the same old way. At times it seems I am getting worse. Furthermore, it is He who is inviting me to follow and unite with Him. I am not starting it. He is. He is the way; He is lighting the way. He is the grace that leads me on.[4] I know so little about this because He doesn't want me to know His mysterious operations within me.

I ask how I can avoid getting so disheartened. Yet it is success that should really surprise me. I have

---

4. Cf. e.g. "Pray as if everything depended on God and work as if everything depended on you"—attributed to St. Ignatius Loyola, cf. Joseph de Guibert, sj, *The Jesuits: Their Spiritual Doctrine and Practice* (Chicago: Loyola University Press, 1964), 148, n. 55. (from *The Catechism of the Catholic Church*, 2834).

to remember that the Lord only enters my heart through the failures that cause my spiritual emptiness. That is where faith comes in. He wants me to be inundated with problems so He can stay with me. Then I will want Him more and more.

I need to be patient with myself. He doesn't get disheartened with me, so why should I get so upset? He loves me just as I am. So why not be myself? He is constantly giving me a chance, so why should I get angry and not give myself a chance?

St. Thomas Aquinas distinguishes patience from forbearance. In *imminentia malorum* and *dilatio bonorum*,[5] he shows that we need patience to tackle tormenting pain, someone's bad conduct, backbiting or wrongdoing. If these things persist I need forbearance. After all, I have to overcome any disheartenment, anger or sadness in the long waiting involved or waiting for ages for something I want very much.

In church we sometimes sing "love is patient," based on 1 Corinthians 13:4. *Patience* in Greek is the definition of forbearance. Only the loving grace

---

5. S.th. I-II, q.136, a.5.

of the Holy Spirit by which Jesus works the miracle of the Consecration is the Architect of my way to God. He encourages me to keep the proper focus so I am on the route until the end. In that hymn, we refer to love's forbearance. It doesn't expect immediate results.

It is often hard for me to be forbearing, as I want everything immediately so that I am better than others. Yet God is not in a hurry. I am the hasty one with an interior hubbub. This impedes my spiritual progress. My impatience may look like zeal or even righteous indignation. I forget that this can be self-love or greed. Yet a silent heart indicates a silent will. To get it in perspective, I need to go to God.

The world would be a different place if we were more patient. I am impatient because of Original Sin. I am full of unrest, while God wants me to have a peaceful heart. "My own peace I give you, a peace that the world cannot give" (Jn. 14:27). This peace also means patience. A peaceful heart is silent.

It is interesting that Jesus greets the Apostles after the Resurrection with the words "Peace be with you!" (Lk. 24:36). These powerful words penetrate anxious hearts shaken up by those dreadful events on Calvary. It looked as though the whole world had collapsed. Jesus says to those frightened, mistrusting hearts: *I bring you peace.* He wants to fill their hearts with faith in His love and power. Forbearance can only be born in the light of believing that God is love and that He is God of the impossible.

I need to avoid disturbingly hurried actions, as He is in charge of everything. I may even experience tragedies. Yet on the Cross and in His Resurrection, He has overcome evil. Our Savior has defeated everything leading to evil, every stress and unrest.

"Peace be with you," we say at Mass; before Communion we ask Him to free us from anxiety. Peaceful hearts receive Him more deeply. Poor reception of Holy Communion needs to be improved through forbearance so that anxieties are removed. He is just now making present the sacrifice to God the Father through the priest and myself. Through His sacrifice He is redeeming us now.

This sacrificial gift returns to me under the Sacred Species. This is the Gift I receive. In Communion, God who sacrificed Himself on the altar a moment earlier, now wants to be a Gift without obstacles in my heart—silent, patient, only waiting for Him.

Nothing is more important than God's coming onto the altar as sacrifice at the Consecration. Later He comes into my heart insofar as I am open to His transforming grace.

Sacrifice should not be separated from Holy Communion. The Church says so. Pope John Paul writes: the Sacrifice, Communion, and Presence are distinct in meaning but united.[6] Faith in the Presence of God living in the Eucharist will help me understand that it is for me that He sacrifices Himself. By faith in His Presence I understand that it is God I receive in this moment. Nothing outweighs this. That is true for us all.

---

6. Cf. John Paul II, the Encyclical Letter *Redemptor hominis*, 20.

So Very Close

I have a distorted picture of God. As I say the Our Father at Mass in a routine sort of way, I don't discover His reality. I usually don't realize that first word *Abba, Father*, allows me to turn to Him with all tenderness: *Abba, Father who loves us, loves me until He is weary.*

. . . You sought me—these words tell about His closeness. God is not at all distant. On the contrary, He is so close that He is ceaselessly taken up with me, especially in the Eucharistic miracle.

My distorted picture of God arises from Original Sin, culture, upbringing, and contemporary society, most of all resistance to grace. I get a proper idea of God from something good that I do in response to His grace; any infidelity, however minimal, deforms this image.

The way to God is through improving my images of Him. St. John of the Cross explains that God has to tackle our illusions. I have to let Him do it.

As faith grows, the pictures get clearer. It is faith that reveals God's reality. I know God loves everybody. Yet saying this can lead to understanding Him to be very far away. It may be a handy concept yet it is incomplete because a metaphysical abstraction. I am saying He loves everybody although I can't imagine the Infinite One. Our Infinite God loves completely differently because for Him, everyone is the only one. To love people is something completely different from loving an individual person. We don't love everybody just as the only one, personally chosen. That is why these statements that "God loves people," "God loves everybody" can sound so abstract and unappealing.

Homilies addressed to the whole congregation tend not to draw an individual. However when the priest speaks to somebody individually, it is much more effective. The disappointment involved in rejecting this is much more acute and calls for something to happen.

With the growth of faith I will gradually discover God's closeness to me personally. I will discover the unique, incomprehensible love of the Eucharistic, hidden God who entirely gives Himself to me very personally.

Tortured so much, scourged, crucified, You rose again. We have been redeemed. The Holy Spirit has descended. The Spirit opens us to the graces of Redemption. We are all rushing somewhere as if God doesn't exist, as if the redemptive graces in every Mass are not waiting for our human hearts to be opened.

Meanwhile, the Dismissal at Mass continues. Our Redeeming God goes on with His quest for hearts very much bound up with the material. The symbolic Sorrowful Christ[7] has greater meaning for today's lost world. God our Redeemer is saddened and concerned for us who are so lost in materialistic preoccupations.

In weariness You sought me. Quaerens me, sedisti lassus.

---

7. Present in Southern Germany, Austria, and Poland.

I will not persevere in seeking deeper conversion without the belief that God personally and exclusively loves me abundantly. Without this conviction, I will fight and resist this truth. I will fear the consequences. Yet my resistance is amazing; I am lukewarm, yielding to temptations and sorrow because of the lack of results, especially spiritual ones. Yet if we listen intently to the voice of grace and hear these amazing words: *Then He, God, loves you with exclusive love; He is for you without any reservation.* Then tears of joy may come. If God Himself loves me so much, nothing is lost. He will not let me be lost. The light will come. Somehow everything will regain its sense.

Yet I can also ask if He really loves a miserable, mean person like me. However, if I remember the truth that He loves me specially, I will not worry so much about the imperfect, objectionable person I can be. Since He loves so much, all is well and it is not too late to respond. If **I really** believe this, my sadness will simply wither away. The conflict is over. He will never give up on me. If I go on being sad, it means I don't believe in the power of His love.

After all, He made me. His love is burning. Benedict XVI confirms this.[8] His love is immeasurably ardent. It is as if I am all He has to love.[9]

That is my undiscovered God. I still don't believe that He loves me in this passionate, supremely caring way. I may not understand how it occurs. I feel lost in the quest. Yet I can know He is constantly caring for me wherever I am.

To be Christian, I need to have a deep appreciation of this vital truth. I am not loved in some abstract, general sort of way. I am loved through and through without any possible reservation just as if **there is nobody and nothing else to love**.

To be a real follower of the Lord I need to be much more alive to this. I mustn't see God as some distant abstraction. To embrace these miraculous truths is to be thoroughly revolutionized. The effect on my life will be outstandingly remarkable.

Perhaps sometimes I will doubt it and rebel. I may even be tempted to think it is not possible to be loved like that. Yet the discovery of this anxiety within me is the very opportunity for me to move

8. Benedict XVI, *Deus caritas est*, 9,10.
9. Cf. ibidem, 10.

toward this real, infinite, constant, ever-present, all-embracing Eucharistic love. It is such a passionate love. It never ceases utterly to quell my deepest fears; its longing for me draws me to ever closer Divine union.

At any stage in the spiritual life, God's Spirit calls me to serve the Church. I am His instrument by means of His life-giving love. Only union with God in love achieves harmonious affinity with and dedication to the Church. According to St. Teresa of Avila, union with God in love is the last stage of the journey toward sanctity. So the final goal of my interior life is not personal sanctification but my complete dedication to the Church, to God's believing Community.

Part II

God's Greatness

A ny importance given to persons and things reduces God's presence and activity within the soul," writes St. John of the Cross.[10] God wants to protect me from being so deeply wrapped up in people and things that I push Him out. Through preoccupation with what He has created, I can effectively cover Him up.

My life will always be quite topsy-turvy if I have more regard for people and things than for our Eucharistic Lord. I can get so wrapped up in my possessions that they begin to take me over to my detriment. I get so drawn away from God that I scarcely relate to the Eucharistic One.

---

10. *"Todo lo que el alma pone en la criatura quita de Dios"*; S. Juan de la Cruz, *Subida del Monte Carmelo*, III,12,1.

I can get so absorbed in my work, it can be like a drug. Workaholics suffer by pushing God out. Results become my spur. In being so attached to them, I marginalize the Eucharist. I don't hand over my concern about the results to Him. That is odd since it is He who determines the outcome.

St. John of the Cross tells us that the more we identify ourselves with things, the more we become subservient to them.[11] I get so wrapped up in my surroundings, I drive God into the outskirts. So we all suffer when the living Eucharistic God actually disappears from my daily life as if He doesn't exist at all.

Fear has big eyes, according to the proverb. What I fear can grow enormously, engulfing me so that both the world and our Eucharistic Redeemer cease to matter in these moments. Yet He is in the Eucharist for me and the world. Fear alone exists and that becomes like an idol for me. My attitude to an idol can either be that of adoring love or fearful rejection.

The more I marginalize God, the more I suffer from fear and haste. It is not just that I need to slow

---

11. Cf. *Ascent of Mount Carmel*, I,4,4.

down. Slowing down can still be haste if I am continually earthbound. Real lack of haste is silence within me. It involves searching for fulfillment in Eucharistic Love. If I am just thirsting for exclusively earthly love, acting very slowly goes on impeding God's grace. Allowing my life to be centered on the One who daily comes onto our altars is the only way to save me from the deprivation of anxiety, sadness, and feverish activity.

I may declare I best find God in nature, yet it is by no means certain I am looking for God in this pastime. It is true that trees are God's gift, yet I can get into a trap if I focus more on them than on God. They can blur my vision, drowning me in the forest by diverting my focus away from the pursuit of amazing Eucharistic Love. I need to avoid making love of nature my final goal. The great and beautiful forest can conceal my Eucharistic, hidden God who is always longing and searching for me.

Where am I going? Should I not change direction? After all, if I receive the grace to believe in the Creator not just of trees and animals but also of galaxies rushing into infinity, then I may get engrossed in His love. It may happen that as I look at the star-filled sky, I will simply pray. I may not be asking for anything but I will be adoring God. Humbly looking in faith includes adoration. Maybe I will be led on beyond the lit-up sky to see my own smallness in contrast to the greatness of the Only One. Maybe I will not just stay with this thought but go on to embrace the inner core of it. Maybe I will hold onto God's greatness in His very personal, supportive power and love. After all, these great things are not just there for me to look at with powerful telescopes. The wonders of the universe are an invitation to draw close to Him in adoring amazement. Everything created should impel me toward incomprehensible Eucharistic Love.

My prayer of adoration should always more or less lead me to God's amazing reality. It is He who is adored in the Eucharist; it is He who is worshiped by choirs of angels. God is always so amazing. However, we need discerning eyes of faith with worshiping hearts inspired by His superabundant miracles. These point to His never-ending love for me. He wants to give me unending opportunities. He wants me to respond at least to some of this truth; He wants me to worship the Eucharist maybe in the words "You are worthy, our Lord and God, to receive glory and honor and power. . ." (Apoc. 4:11). He superabundantly reveals His glory to inspire me to some adoration of the real Master of the Universe. On the Eucharistic altar He always reigns supreme.

I still minimize the King of the Universe. In my everyday life I undervalue the Eucharistic One. Yet my participation in the Mass is a vital part of my life. I frequently ask how it is that I don't make the Infinite One more important, especially on account of His miraculously incomprehensible Eucharistic love. Why don't I change in a radical way? I am everything to Him; I am the one who is unique to Him; He just wants me to share in His eternal glory.

The Language
of the Elements

Faith leads me to see more of God's presence in the world and its phenomena. That is true even in the havoc of terrifying tsunamis destroying life, houses, hotels, cemeteries, and forests.

God is present in the scorching sun and droughts; He is present in unexpected torrential rain and destructive floods; He is even present as we are rescued just because we held onto the remains of our furniture. We are terrified and shocked in the face of such events. We get so taken up with saving ourselves and others, we can forget all about God. We have unconsciously reduced His Dominion and power. These increasing catastrophes reveal our lack of faith.

It was similar for the Israelites. They were terrified by pursuing Egyptian chariots. God seemed powerless and immaterial. They were panic-stricken. Ours is not a world of chariots but of bomb explosions, scorching droughts, and domineering floods. The voice of Jesus the Savior says, "If you have faith, you could. . ." (cf. Mt. 17:20).

Increasing catastrophes should remind me of God's presence. His voice says: *Look, I am so insignificant. You are not even thinking of Me. You don't hear or understand what I am saying in these events. You separate them from Me. How can I help you since you don't need Me, since you want to face the elements on your own?*

I simply don't believe God can halt tsunamis. I think there is no such power to stop destructive hurricanes: *Calm down!*

God wants to perform miracles. We stop Him by our lack of faith. The Storm at Sea involving the Apostles (cf. Mt. 8:24–27) was less than today's disasters. Yet the point is the same. Jesus only waited so that they could share their helpless-ness with Him. The fearful crying involved hardly any faith. Yet God doesn't expect great faith from me. If only I listened to His whisper in these world catastrophes, perhaps I would hear: *Why are you so afraid, you of little faith?* (cf. Mt. 8:26). *Why don't you come to this little tabernacle where I am locked up for you? The world's history takes place here; your history takes place here too.*

Will these disasters cease? Through their power He tells me that they are nothing compared with His almighty power. Moreover, these catastrophes expose the truth that God is still too insignificant for me. Yet in big or small experiences, God whispers: *Believe Me, Lord of the World. Believe that I am really present on the world's altars. To calm the hurricanes and storms, I just need your faith. I have the power to stop the floods. I, your God, am hidden in the Eucharist. Are you convinced of God's power?*

Highly worrying events demonstrate God's love for us. He is constantly calling for faith. He is calling us to recognize His significance in it all.

My helplessness in these situations exposes my lack of faith. So I am given the right to implore His mercy. I need to implore it to receive the Eucharistic sacrament of faith. Our Eucharistic Savior longs to revive my shaky, limping faith.

We need just a fragment of contrition in our misery to release His Love. My real misery is my constantly forgetting Him. Being lost prepares me for the Eucharist. I desperately need His love in these threatening situations so that I can ask for His constant action in me. I can be filled with His inviting grace if I offer no resistance. Moreover, that will be unique for me. It can turn the course of history. In such events, I can gain much more confidence in Him by losing my inflated self-confidence. His acts within me can then become pure acts of love. As St. John of the Cross mentions, such events can be the occasion of extraordinary interior transformation with a greater significance than all the deeds in the Church put together.[12]

You never cease searching for me, Jesus . . . so that I can allow You to find me and eventually be filled with Your Eucharistic Love.

---

12. Cf. *The Spiritual Canticle*, 29,2.

Demolition
of Hippo

In 430, eighty thousand Vandals and Alans commanded by King Gaiseric attacked Hippo, Algeria, the See of St. Augustine. The outstanding Father of the Church was engrossed, writing about grace. St. Augustine's last days were very bitter and painful.

The siege lasted fourteen months, culminating in the city's being burnt down. Hippo was destroyed in two stages. In the beginning, Arian defenders of Hippo—soldiers of Bonifacius, the Emperor's governor in Africa—were attacking the city from inside. Finally it was burned by the invading Arian Vandals. Augustine witnessed abandoned churches and the expulsion of dedicated virgins. It was all very painful. Surviving churches were deserted.

There were no services or sacraments; Arianism prevailed.

The defeat seemed complete. Yet there is no defeat with God. These are occasions for Hope. Although St. Augustine's world collapsed, it was just the collapse of human reliances. Anyway, in the light of faith these were illusory. God and His grace are always there. This merciful grace is uniquely abundant when structures, institutions, possessions, plans, and desires collapse. Augustine witnessed this world's passing glory (cf. 1 Cor. 7:31b). God and His grace always remain. That was why his last writings were about grace. As Hippo fell, he only thought of building up Christian conviction. That means relying on God's merciful grace rather than our own ability.

This was a period of huge revolutions. 410 appears as the turning point when Alaric's Visigoths destroyed the walls of Rome, capital of the whole civilized world. Rome had been deemed indestructible. This was a period of great migrations because of the constant barbarian invasions. There was great fear. Foundations were collapsing everywhere.

When our world collapses, we can either be totally self-reliant or we can seek support in God's grace. Augustine was no hero. He knew that as long as he relied on his own strength, he was on a downward path. He was only saved by special graces. He had uniquely discovered the gift of grace. He didn't feel heroic or great before God. The effects of his sins haunted him long after his conversion. He still had temptations to sensuality and conceit due to much public praise. He was highly esteemed and valued. After so many years of work and prayer he still saw his imperfections. This proves his authentic sanctity. His misery was so great that he never thought of himself as saintly.

If I endlessly multiply religious practices or want to serve God with the idea that He only demands my good deeds to merit His admiration, I am on the verge of twisted faith. I lack real union with God. If, however, I have discovered that the God of good deeds first of all seeks me, wanting to live in me, then I am following Augustine. He never forgot how much he had been forgiven, even forty-four years after conversion. During the siege of Hippo, eleven days before his death, he shut himself in to be alone with the merciful Lord. He arranged for parchments to be put on his bedroom walls with the penitential psalms written on them in big letters. Reading them, the Doctor of grace regretted his sinful life.

If I long for union with God, various things in my life collapse. Everything depends on my attitude. Augustine didn't lament all this. It is not worth crying over this world. Openness to the Eucharist helps insofar as I believe that, as St. Paul says, ". . . the form of this world is passing away" (1 Cor. 7:31).

In the besieged city, Augustine kept close to God. He didn't lament the loss of Hippo or his great achievements. It was just God and he. Everything else he saw as illusory. Sooner or later we become dust. It came home to him through this seclusion before his death. He had left everybody and everything. His only goals were truth, contrition, and the grace of greater union with God.

If he were attached to what he had done, he would have lamented this. Everything was now departing into darkness. Yet it appears from his *Confessions* that he had no notion that he had done something very important or become saintly. He died joyfully contrite, knowing God had forgiven him.

As I leave this world, the Eucharist is everything. There is nothing to weep about. If the Eucharist is my treasure, I can leave the world happily. Everything I do in my life is only a means. It falls apart just like St. Augustine's diocese. After all, a local church may fall apart. Jesus assures indestructibility only to the Church as a whole. Particular churches have no such assurance.

A lost treasure is what causes us to lament. If the Eucharist is my treasure, I will not weep over material losses. *The shape of this world is constantly changing.* To lament over material losses is to lament over illusions.

St. Augustine's purification was severe. Hippo, into which he had put so much loving effort, had collapsed. What had taken years to build was destroyed. The Vandals went on to invade for another hundred years. Such was the fate of one of the greatest Christian saints and Church Fathers.

Hippo is today the harbor city Annaba in Algeria. There is just of a handful of worshipers in a building that serves as a cathedral. Humanly speaking, everything was destroyed. Yet God never loses. Maybe the destruction of Hippo was necessary so that St. Augustine could find deeper union with God. In place of his destroyed city, the Lord erected the invisible building of St. Augustine's soul. The Church there was upheld for many centuries more. It still draws inspiration from Augustine's life and work.

If I treasure memories of what I do for God, I am under an illusion. Christ didn't shed His Precious Blood for Hippo. He did it for His beloved Augustine. Therefore it is not important to think about what I leave behind. After me there is only what God built in me. God saved St. Augustine from seeing demolition and conflagration. He was just allowed deeply important acts of sorrow.

I need to get this straight. Perhaps in my feverish activity and the Hippo consideration I begin to realize that God, who comes to me in the Eucharist, makes me the important issue. He doesn't want my works. He wants me. He wants to conquer me for His glory.

I don't have to think of what I will leave behind. He decides that. Nothing else matters. The more I lose this passing earthly life, like the loss of Hippo, the better. One thing is important. I need humbly to receive my loving, Eucharistic Lord. That is enough for me. God, united with me in Holy Communion, can only dwell in me when like Augustine, I have nothing else. When I yearn to *expect His coming in glory.*

Part III

In Weariness You
Seek Me

She is hiding among the trees, running away
from him. He is looking for her. Their whole
joy is in this hide-and-seek. Actually they would
both like her to run for as long as possible. That is
because when he finds her, she runs to a different
part of the forest so he will look for her again.

It is rather like this with the Lord. He is hiding so
I can seek him. He is hiding under the Eucharistic
species, hoping I will find Him with ever-greater
eagerness. God is hiding because love always
seeks.

Like the seasons, our emotions are constantly
changing. We stop seeking and then the drama
begins. When faith, hope, and love lessen, Jesus in

the Eucharist brings them to life again. He tries to inspire us to seek Him. He promotes falling in love with this seeking. Seeking is finding; finding is seeking.[13] To find God is to seek Him. The principle of the interior life is seeking, not finding. Seeking always finds. Yet as St. Gregory of Nyssa tells us, we are always starting.[14]

"If you knew the gift of God" (Jn. 4:10). The Samaritan woman came to Jesus crushed by her sin, so she was subconsciously longing to meet Jesus. She had no idea who was waiting for her. The One with whom she was so impressed, revealed Himself to remove scales from her eyes.

Every meeting with God is prayer. It is a meeting of the unworthy with the Highest Light. He wants to remove scales from eyes to make Himself known. God reveals Himself in prayer insofar as I look for Him. Yet He makes the first move.

When I go to Mass, I am like the Samaritan woman. I go to get something. Everything seems so ordinary for me, yet nothing is more important. Similarly with the Samaritan woman. Carrying

---

13. Cf. St. Gregory of Nyssa, *Homiliae in Canticum*, 8 PG 44,941 C.
14. Ibidem.

water was relatively unimportant. Christ Himself looks for somebody unprepared like her. He first speaks, asking for a drink. I don't seek Him. He is already waiting, thirsting for me: "his speaking arises from the depths of God's desire for us."[15]

My participation in the Mass, whether I realize it or not, fulfills God's desire and my own. Yet my desire may be hidden and faint. Maybe I am just out to fulfill my obligation. Yet there is still some desire. God longs for me to want Him "If you knew the gift of God, . . . you would have asked Him, and he would have given you living water" (Jn. 4:10).

Quaerens me, sedisti lassus—in weariness you sought me. . . .[16] *Unexpectedly You come to me in these words. You come with your silence and peace. Silence and peace—light flows from these words. It is as if they captivate and transfer me to a different reality— the reality of Your offering of Yourself. Wanting to move me to faith, You tell me Your love speaks simply; someone who has lost a loved one, seeks for him. Afterwards he is nigh exhausted.*

---

15. *The Catechism of the Catholic Church*, 2560.

16. The verse coming from the sequence read in the Divine Office of the last week of the Church Year.

All this isn't just about anybody. It is about You, God who accepted human nature so I could understand things. You long for me. Your humanity brings me to the truth of Your extraordinary love. As God You do not get weary; yet on earth, sharing our human nature, You cried and got tired. All for me personally. I am not running after You. You are chasing me by Your love or just by Your Voice. You seek me because Your very seeking marvelously exposes my needs.

Quaerens me, sedisti lassus—words that speak of You and me; about me, constantly lost in life's avenues, whom You desperately need to find. That is how You are saving me. You bring me hope as I know You are never giving up the pursuit. So I place my hope in Your searching. My peace comes from that. It tells me that finally I will not go astray.

I am guilty of losing You by going away from You. I forget You love me exclusively. My thoughts, desires, and likings are miles away. In avoiding you, I get lost.

No matter what happens to me, no matter how far I stray away, You never give up the search. You never weary of me even with my fleeting absences. You, the Divine Searcher of the lost, eagerly come looking for me. You are unaware of any fatigue.

You unceasingly love me. You reveal it by constantly looking for me in the Eucharist. You keep injecting me with Eucharistic grace so that Your redeeming, suffering exhaustion is not in vain. From the Eucharistic altar You can lift me, heal me, and constantly tell me about Your incomprehensible love for me.

You bring me hope that eventually Your tirelessness will amaze me so much, I will be secure in the thought that I will never leave You again. The time will come when You will not have to seek me anymore. Your tiredness will be over, not because I will have changed but because Your searching will begin to affect me so deeply that I will never want to leave You. You will have finally found me. I thank You. I only thank You for the peace it brings me. It is only You who find.

I am thinking that someday, in keeping with Your wish, I will discover Eucharistic love and be taken up with You who unceasingly love me. Your Eucharistic love will deeply penetrate my life, purifying me. In this Eucharistic way You will always fill me with Yourself. Someday You will introduce me to the light of Your glory that always waits for me.

Two Realities

We are surrounded by the two realities of infinite Love and . . . destructive Hatred. Although so strong, hatred is finite. Yet in the face of it, I am inconceivably weak.[17] Because I believe I can manage life on my own, I am unconsciously influenced by the power of the destructive real one who is **Hatred**. The only real existing Power is God, who[18] infinitely loves me. Yet He doesn't want to force Himself when I am self-sufficient in turning my back on Him. When I do that, the power of God's love becomes pretty defenseless. His loving hands constantly wait to catch hold of me. If I treat them

---

17. Cf. *The Catechism of the Catholic Church*, 2854.
18. Cf. *The Catechism of the Catholic Church*, 395.

as if they don't exist, I continually insult that incomprehensible loving concern for me.

So I am defenseless before this destructive Hatred always so near to me. It is incredibly alert and active ". . . and the whole world is in the power of the evil one" (1 Jn. 5:18–19). If I don't believe in the prince of this world, I will not believe in his ingenious temptations. I will not bother with those words "Your adversary the devil prowls around like a roaring lion, seeking someone to devour. Him withstand, being firm in your faith" (1 Pet. 5:8–9). I will constantly fall. I will be similar to a man looking for water in the desert when it is right next to him. I am so close to the saving spring, yet I am searching everywhere because the Adversary invents various mirages before my eyes. He shows me beautiful oases with trees and bushes that obscure life-giving water. I chase after them. When it turns out to be false, another mirage appears—an oasis full of palms and luxuriant vegetation. I rush again. The real oasis is still so near. Yet the Adversary wants me to miss it by looking elsewhere.

I need to believe that this power of Hatred is constantly with me. It always disguises itself as something good. If I don't believe this to be destructive Hatred, continually disguising itself as something good, I will not be able to return from this lost pathway.

The Parable of the Prodigal Son describes it well. It tells of the prodigal's illusory mirages about the far country to which he went. We are all prodigal[19] and tempted to go away from the true oasis into the dried up desert. We follow illusory oases. Many sufferings come from it all. Yet the youngest son was always at the spring, living so close to his father, the symbol of God's amazing love.

Prodigal children keep doing it. We are all lost prodigal sons and daughters. We are all driven to desire *to possess or be something more.* In consequence the desire grows stronger and stronger. Personal Hatred comes quickly to say, "Look, I will give you all you are looking for. I will give you something *to increase your stature and possessions."*

If I believed in the existence of this destructive Hatred, I would believe I am being **constantly**

---

19. John Paul II, *Reconciliatio et paenitentia*, 5.

51

tempted. Then I might be on the watch. In Gethsemane, the Lord uttered those words for us all, "Watch and pray that you may not enter into temptation" (Mt. 26:41a). Christ calls me to be on the alert, by which I may understand that he calls me to be on my guard against this Hatred: *Believe in it. Be on the watch. You are constantly being tempted.*

Who really believes he is **constantly** tempted and weak in the face of it? I am tiny beside this power of Hatred. I am very small, yet I believe in myself. Believing so much in myself I become increasingly vulnerable.

A chain of temptations and evil surrounds me to help break down the only true power of infinite Love. The power of this Love defeated the evil prince of this world by His death and resurrection. Yet He still desires and searches for me.

In weariness You sought me. Seeking me, You would like to tell me: If you believed in this Hatred, you would take fright. Yet it appears so good, beautiful, and magnificent. Belief in this Hatred means revealing its perverse actions to you. You would see there is only one way out—to believe in Infinite Love,

Goodness, and Beauty. This Power and Love are freely locked up and abandoned in the tabernacles of the world. This Love freely hides its majesty from me. I have to force my way to God through the only means of faith.

This Love is constantly granting me the grace of faith. Everything depends on me: I am free to accept or reject this Eucharistic gift. If I accept it, I will see the most extraordinary miracle of the world on the altar. I will see this Love that is giving its life for me in this very moment: "this is My Body, which **is given up** for you."[20] "This is the cup of My Blood, the Blood of the new and everlasting covenant. **It is shed** for you and for all so that sins may be forgiven"—now.

It is *now* when my Redemption is being accomplished. *Now* I am at the source of all graces, being given the greatest of God's gifts. This Eucharistic participation gives me everything I need. I will receive all this because of God's plan. *Now* on the altar He gives His life for me. Only He can distinguish which desires are good or bad for me.

---

20. In the original Greek version the words of consecration are used in the present tense. Cf. Mt. 26:28, Lk. 22:19.

Hatred is everywhere. Even during the Eucharist I am somehow tempted without knowing it.

The Blessed Sacrament is God Himself giving Himself. He in His sacrifice, in His real presence comes inside me and wants to permeate my whole being with even a particle of His life, to illuminate it. The Eucharist is light bringing light. It wants to illuminate me with God's incomprehensible love, extraordinarily revealing Himself in this sacrament. However, even after I receive this Sacrament, some areas of darkness remain in me.

How do I defend myself against the temptation and open up to Eucharistic saving graces? Only by being small. Hatred cannot stand such attitudes. It always builds illusory, elevated thrones. Since I am blind to it, my pride induces me to build these illusory thrones at the behest of the prince of this world. I have always to be small especially when I am in church before the tabernacle or when I am at Mass. The prince of this world fears humility. He knows that when I am small I stand in the truth. The whole power of Love surrounds me. He fears this and has to run away.

If I am small, there is an absence of the aura of coveted greatness. The Eucharistic Jesus is able to live in me because I will finally have opened my heart to Him in my tormented wandering. I will then be amazed to see that when I was astray, I was being looked for by that Love that never abandons me. Finally I will have opened myself to It, and It will be able fully to conquer me for Its glory.

Lord Jesus, Come in Glory

That was an astonishing miracle Jesus performed among the Gerasenes (cf. Mk. 5:1–20). The unfortunate possessed man cried out day and night, gashing himself with stones. Among those tombs and in the mountains, he terrified everybody. They felt completely helpless in the face of it all. Jesus liberated them. Amazed, they witnessed a man unable to control himself, who tore off his shackles and chains, now sitting peacefully and happily before the Lord.

However, it is quite clear they were unappreciative. They would have held on to Jesus ardently if they had been thanking Him for this extraordinary miracle that freed the man from such awful suffering. On the contrary, they simply asked Him to go away as soon as possible. They were more concerned about losing their pigs that raced into the lake than God's miraculous power. Their interest was in pigs, not God.

The rich young man also had his pigs. He feared losing them, so he rejected Jesus. The Gerasenes were admittedly not Israelites like him; they pastured pigs that the Israelites considered to be impure animals. Yet this stunning miracle left them unmoved. They could only think of their pigs.

In every man there is the real and ideal ego. Ideal ego is that secret part of me bound up with some deep desire or hope. All of us can relate to this. It is those secret, hidden dreams; it is what I would like to be in my heart of hearts. The Gerasenes were not expecting God. They preferred God's messenger to go away and leave them with their pigs.

It is so easy after the Consecration to say: ". . . Lord Jesus, come in glory," since in this moment I offer the best aspect of my ego to God. *Yes, I await Your coming in glory and may my pigs fall into the lake with all the lusts, desires, worldly pursuits I want to keep secret.*

Do I really realize that all this may fall into the lake if I really *await His coming in glory?* In these words I radically chose God. *All of me awaits Your coming.* The more I am open to these words, the more I am open to the Savior God's miraculous ways. *Most importantly, You, Jesus, are alive on the altar. The pigs may die in the lake as I expect Your coming today, now, the day that brings Your last coming closer. You alone, Eucharistic Jesus, are the hope and sense in my life. Without You I couldn't live.*

I trust that this liturgical prayer "Lord Jesus, come in glory" will grow more and more in my heart as I wait for Your coming to become part of my daily life; that it becomes part of my life owned by You.

The expectation of the Lord's second coming is deeply ingrained in the Mass. After the consecration of the wine, we address Jesus, proclaiming His death and professing His resurrection "until You come again."[21] In these words, we hear *Marana tha*, "Come Lord Jesus!" that rang out during those first centuries' Eucharistic celebrations. In the light of

---

21. The original Polish used these words from the former Mass text: "In the words: '. . . Lord Jesus, come in glory' we hear *Marana tha*. . . ."

the Lord's second coming, the "glory" of earthly life should fade before my eyes. In the light of His glory, my worries need to fade away. Problems should eat into me much less because *He will come in glory*. All worries will become absurd.

These words inspire conversion. If I sincerely bring these things to God present on the altar, if I sincerely join the ensuing prayer: "and ready to greet him when he comes again, we offer you in thanksgiving this holy and living Sacrifice," I will remember that this offering of Sacrifice grows in me according to my expectation. It introduces me to a different reality.

The Church once again refers to this hope when it prays before Communion, ". . . as we await the blessed hope and the coming of our Savior, Jesus Christ." His coming in Communion is the preparation for that other coming. Holy Communion is given to hope for the Lord's second coming. This is our hopeful faith.

This important hope introduces me into a different world, not this one with so much evil, unlawfulness, and pain but God's, permeated with that triple truth of His death, resurrection, and coming glory. He will come to me in glory. Just for me He is now offering the Holy Sacrifice to remove the areas of my personal remaining darkness.

I often forget that the Eucharistic eschatological dimensions are extremely important. They involve my need for conversion through pursuit of personal Eucharistic Love. As so few expect His coming, so few prepare for it. He will come in glory, but how will this sudden coming find me? Concentrating on Him in interior silence? Or maybe preferring earthly illusions, keeping the pigs from running into the lake. Expecting His coming in glory means desiring Him now as King of my heart. *In every step I take, in my writing, in the car, I expect Your coming in glory, leading me into eternal glory.*

I need to work as if this world will not pass away. Yet I need to live as if I am to die tomorrow, not as if I will never die. I have to be ready to meet the Lord. This needs to be my focus.

As soon as Jesus comes onto the altar at the Consecration, the Church makes me expect His next coming. One Christian thinker tells of a vision concerning the Lord's second coming. He saw the priest raising the Host after the consecration and suddenly the end arrived. Out of this elevated Host emerges Christ in His whole glory, surrounded by Angels.

In faith I should immediately try to discover the Angels' choirs surrounding the altar. The Eucharistic celebration is participation in heavenly liturgy. Angels cannot leave Jesus, for whom they were created.[22] In the First Eucharistic Prayer, the priest, just after the Consecration, bowing in the name of the Church, utters the amazing words: "almighty God: command that these gifts be borne by the hands of your holy Angel to your altar on high. . . ."

Your glory is revealed when I offer no resistance to Your grace. You find Your glory in sanctifying those whom You love dearly, for whom You shed blood on the cross. "Lord Jesus, come in glory" means that I should have the beginning of a desire to see by faith the Angels around the altar along with my yearning for heaven.

The more sincerely I say these words, the more my focus will increase. They ask: Do I really want His coming in glory, now? Am I ready for this

---

22. Cf. *The Catechism of the Catholic Church*, 33, 1090.

coming? Do I expect it? I should try not to be terrified by the thought of His coming or afraid of its disturbing my private world. I should try mentally to live that reality. For this glory will have to recreate my own earthly world and transform it into something new.

After all, Jesus coming in glory will involve a new heaven and earth, not this earth to which I desperately cling. There will be a new earth and heaven. The words: ". . . Lord Jesus, come in glory" invite me radically to change my outlook. They invite me to want to bring the Lord's coming closer to earth and heaven here and now. *Faith already makes it clear that You, my Eucharistic God, wish to embrace me forever in Your incomprehensible glory.*

Part IV

You Need My Silence

It is in silence that God, from whom I so regularly turn away, comes to me. For God is Silence. He comes and speaks in silence. I am full of interior noise. I am full of noisy desires, passions, and curiosity. I always want to know and see more, as the more I know, the more I am esteemed.

There is no real silence in me. I keep on uttering needless words, asking needless questions. I am too focused on what is unnecessary. This all distracts me from my Eucharistic God. He can't be in touch or talk to me when I am like this. "After you have left everything," says St. Thérèse, invoking the *Imitation of Christ,* "you must above all leave yourself."[23]

---

23. St. Thérèse of the Child Jesus, *Letter to Céline*, 2 August 1893.

Curiosity may seem irrelevant. Yet in striving to keep interior silence, small insignificant things are important. Curiosity about the world, human affairs, and everyday happenings can be a big obstacle in my spiritual pursuit. I need to find calmness in my excessive attachment to exterior things. This mustn't, however, lessen my awareness of people in need of help. The curiosity that needs curbing works in me like a constantly switched-on TV. I may not have a TV, yet needless curiosity acts as if there is one switched on inside me all the time.

I can reject this Silence by the noise of pushy pride, excessively wanting to please others. This is often a terrible enslavement, confusing my spiritual endeavors. Perhaps blinded by habitually acting like this, I see it as something quite different.

Haste is interior noise. I am always chasing after something; I tend always to be on the go or clock-watching. Yet if I try to reduce my driving speed for God, it becomes a prayer. If I try to let God slow me down, He can take me over. Becoming interiorly silent creates the conditions for the Silent One to come to me. My haste is a nasty thing, destroying my bond with Him who is all for me. My haste simply pushes Him away.

Haste also destroys the body. God's passionate love can speak to me through my body as it disintegrates, loses resistance, or becomes worn out with age. Maybe I will get to understand that my sufferings and illnesses have a lot to do with my haste. As I leave the Silence of God, I am highly prone to enter the sick world, the area of tormenting sicknesses. So through ignoring God, which involves ignoring proper care of the body, many contemporary illnesses like backache, circulatory problems, allergies, and tumors arise in this feverish, senseless running around. Opposed to the silence of God are haste and anxiety induced by over-ambitious images of personal greatness.

We so much need interior silence. To find everything, we need to want nothing and nobody outside Him. Yet even this depends on being in touch with His will. Fulfilling God's will brings us to discover that this is the pathway to our salvation, soul and body. It promotes love in every direction.

It is not always possible to pray mentally and with feeling. The inner light of faith where God lives doesn't always reach the outskirts. Most important is silence of will, interior quietness, a certain form of detachment when my will focuses overwhelmingly on Him. Then I supremely desire His will, seek His presence, and want to serve Him. When everything else ceases to have immediate value for me, my will and love are paradoxically enriched in every direction and concern. Without this, there is neither interior silence nor good prayer.

Silence of will involves not planning too much. I can find it by taking up the challenge of having more flexible plans. By silence I am ready to have my plans thwarted. Yet I am aware how much confusion and anxiety every disappointment causes me. This is one of the biggest obstacles to finding real peace.

God pointedly says to my always being on the go, intense and full of my own plans: *Look, I remain present for you in the "Sacrament of silence." All this noise, rushing around, tension, and enslavement to self will obscure My Eucharistic Presence. Your sadness, anxiety, and haste impede your communion of life with Me. I so much need your interior silence. I need the silence of your will so that you only want Me.*

Your sadness, anxiety, and haste can all be subjected to redemption if you open yourself to me in the Sacrament of My Love. Give Me those busy tensions destroying your soul and body. Allow Me once more to forgive you everything on the altar in My redemptive Eucharistic Sacrifice. I can then convince you again that there is no love like Mine.

Jesus's Tears

God's Love is all embracing. It includes most faithful friends but even somebody who turns out to be like Judas.

That is how it is with our incomprehensible Eucharistic God. His love excludes nobody. Pope Benedict XVI says it is simultaneously *agape* and *eros.*[24]

In the Gospels we see that Jesus wept and was moved to tears. "Truly, truly, I say to you, one of you will betray Me" (Jn. 13:21). Maybe He wept as He said this of Judas. God's love couldn't conceivably exclude Judas, who betrayed Him. Judas knew this; he had seen Jesus's tears.

---

24. Cf. the Encyclical Letter *Deus caritas est*, 9-10.

If my sin weighs on me and I feel I am lacking faith and God's love, I can hear the Gospel words in the Mass. The invisible Jesus, in whom I have lost trust, is crying for me. Maybe Judas didn't notice this. Man only sees what he wants to see.

The Gospels tell us Jesus wept over Jerusalem: "And when he drew near and saw the city he wept over it, saying, 'Would that even today you knew the things that make for peace! but now they are hid from your eyes. For the days will come upon you, when your enemies will cast up a bank about you and surround you, and hem you in on every side, and dash you to the ground, you and your children within you, and they will not leave one stone upon another in you; because you did not know the time of your visitation'" (Lk. 19:41–44).

Jesus also cries when He shares other people's pains. He empathized with the faithful Mary of Bethany whom He dearly loved. "When Jesus saw her weeping . . ., he was deeply moved in spirit and troubled" (Jn. 11:33). Jesus was moved by her grief.

I need to find this love, loving through thick and thin, not wavering despite betrayal and rejection.

Jesus wasn't accepted in Jerusalem; He cries over human pain.

Even though He knew He would bring Lazarus back to life, Our Lord shared Mary's grief. In the face of suffering, He wasn't indifferent to her tears. His empathy was outstanding.

In a sense, Jesus caused her pain and tears. Despite knowing of Lazarus's sickness—"Lord, he whom you love is ill"—He "stayed two days longer in the place where he was" (Jn. 11:3, 6). She knew it too: "Lord, if You had been here, my brother would not have died" (Jn. 11:32). Even though she was thinking in a purely human way, Jesus respectfully came. He knew she didn't know God's plans involved the delay in His coming to grieve with her. She had a big trial of faith. He knows best. That trial of faith was very painfully necessary. It all reveals God's glory with clarity. This restoration to life lights up every detail so that many would come to believe in Him.

Maybe all these events occurred to inspire Mary of Bethany, so much loved by Jesus, toward even greater affection. She discovers His Love. He is touched by her tears. Afterward He restores everything. Her beloved brother was with her once more.

All these things give us an insight into some of the depths of God's ways. Despite all Mary's love, something was standing in the way—she missed her brother's support. Through it all, she drew nearer to the Source and Origin of Love. The detaching, renewing course of events marvelously purified all her love. That is the Lord's mission.

Six days before Passover, Jesus's love brought Him to Bethany again. Mary was now totally with Jesus. She was strongly focused on Him rather than Lazarus, Martha, or the Apostles. She knelt at His feet, pouring oil onto them and wiping them with her hair. She had discovered His love. He had become everything for her. Her closer focus on Divine Love naturally improved the quality of her love for everything and everybody. His love completely absorbed all her worldly concerns.

Like Mary of Bethany, Judas received everything. It is valuable to compare the two emotional experiences to see the contrast of His Love for the faithful and the unfaithful. Jesus weeps over the very faithful and the very unfaithful.

So I begin to see universal Love and some of its depths. This love is not found through knowledge. Each of us vitally needs to discover this here and now, not just in theory.

This opportunity is always in the Eucharist. He is here and now loving me whether I am following the way of Mary of Bethany or Judas. His Love is incomprehensible. As my life goes on its intricate ways, I don't even realize where I am. In fact I walk somewhere in between both pathways. Partially with Mary, partially with Judas. It is only in the Eucharistic Jesus that I find the necessary vision. I need to be open to it.

It is only in Jesus that I find it all. My attitude to Him is pivotal. It is only with Him that I can get it right. Every moment is a choice. I may chose or reject Him. Our Eucharistic Jesus is always at our side, yet not of course in the choice of evil. If I am lost with nobody to turn to, He is there weeping with me. As glorified now on the altar, He doesn't cry, but I can't forget His outstanding humanity.

Revelation enlightens my confused conscience. By it I see Jesus both in the abstraction of *agape* and the palpable *eros*.[25] I move closer to Jesus as I combine these two aspects of love. Between transubstantiation and Communion in the Mass there is the reality of Eucharistic Jesus, the God-Man who comes onto the altar by the power of the Holy Spirit in the words of consecration. It is this Jesus who in Holy Communion comes to sinful me. Actually it is He who receives me. Whether I come to Him like Judas or more like Mary of Bethany, I always come as sinner.

After all, Mary's weeping like that over her brother's death was a sign of her need for more faith. She treasured her brother. She had lost somebody she loved. Yet it is only through increasing faith that our love improves and matures. In the light of faith, a brother is more of a treasure because by it we see God's presence in him. Faith removes illusions. St. Paul says: *Those who have family, who have brother or sister, should live as though they had none, because the fashion of this world is passing away* (cf. 1 Cor. 7:29–31). It is passing away. The lasting reality is Eucharistic Jesus.

Mary's tears were very much to do with her loss. This revealed some of her infidelity to the Lord

---

25. Cf. Pope Benedict XVI, *Deus caritas est*, 9-10.

and her need for the balm of increasing faith. Our Eucharistic Lord is always Bread for the unfaithful, for sinners, even if they feel like saints. She wasn't yet a saint. It is only when the Holy Spirit penetrates her being, sanctifying her with His extraordinary grace, that faithful Mary sees how in her pain she was without enough trust. That pain wasn't so necessary after all. God can give her everything—Himself and what she had lost. It had seemed she had lost so much. Jesus wanted to tell her that when she chooses **Him**, everything is restored to her, including Lazarus. Now she has her affection for Lazarus in correct perspective. Lazarus will never again be so important to her that the Lord is overshadowed.

Only Say the Word...

Jesus uttered provocative words to the man who asked for his son to be healed from epilepsy. The man had said, "If you can do anything, have pity on us and help us." Jesus replied: "If You can?" He is amazed by the disbelief despite His frequent and numerous miracles: "All things are possible to him who believes!" (cf. Mk. 9:22–23). For the believer, God can do everything. Even Judas could have been rescued if like that father he had cried out: "I believe, help my unbelief" (Mk. 9:24). Even an unbeliever turning to Him, admitting the disbelief, is helped. He asks us to refrain from putting obstacles to His power.

We need more than to believe in God's love. We also need to believe in His power. Then we discover Jesus in His peace and happiness—only then.

Jesus is amazed by the centurion's request, "Lord, I am not worthy to have You come under my roof; but only say the word, and my servant will be healed" (Mt. 8:8). That is faith in His power. Somewhere in the background there is also faith in His love. The centurion, seeing so many miracles happening, was somehow touched by the Lord's mercy. He then needed some belief in this Heart that pitied human misery. His faith was extraordinary. There was no lack of faith in Jesus's goodness among the Jews. They lacked faith in His power.

The Apostles noticed the Master's emotional sorrow for the crowds. They believed in His love. However, the centurion's faith in His power is expressed in military terms: "For I also am a man under authority, having soldiers under me. And I say to this one, Go, and he goes; and to another, Come, and he comes" (Mt. 8:9). A soldier has to obey his officers. The centurion understands that nature's laws obey Jesus. He knows He doesn't even have to come in person. He doesn't need to touch to heal.

He knows that His power can operate even from a distance. "Truly I say to you, with no one in Israel have I found such great faith" (Mt. 8:10). These words of astonishment come from God Himself.

It is vital to believe in God's power that may be revealed at any moment. Faith in His love will not suffice because love can be helpless. Love that cries and sympathizes is for sure an extraordinary love. That is not enough for us. We need more than sympathy. We need God Himself. It is only when we discover that God's love is power that we really desire Him. The Lord's love is inseparable from His power.

Power and love are just one infinite thing for Him. It always wants to save me through the Eucharist. It is effective according to my openness. It is only belief in Jesus that impedes evil. I need to believe in His infinite power. Otherwise sin takes over.

If my life is going in the direction of Judas Iscariot, I am just aware of Jesus's tears. I can wrongly see them as weakness. This can be the basic reason for my wrongful ways. Judas didn't connect the Lord's emotion with His infinite Power. So there was no miracle. Mary of Bethany, on the contrary, recognized that unity. So a great miraculous event took place. His Love revealed His Power.

Like us, Mary was human and couldn't be expected to know the whole state of affairs. He had to accommodate His Infinite power and love to what we humans see as the miracle of rising from the dead. It sufficed and had to be sufficient for Mary. She couldn't foresee His glory. He told her what she needed to know. Anything more could have destroyed her. After all, He loved her so much. Thus in raising Lazarus from the dead, He curtailed the revelation of His glory. For her and for those who came later to see her brother, it was an extraordinary sign of Jesus's power, inspiring faithful greater acceptance of Him.

God's love and power have to be revealed to me little by little, according to my abilities. Yet this has to be with sufficient inspiration so that I may grow out of my wrongly focused, excessive worldly attachments and perseveringly forever be under the inspiration of Almighty Love.

At Holy Communion I say: "Lord, I am not worthy that you should enter my roof, but only say the word and my soul shall be healed." For a while I am aware of some truth about my unfaithful frequent weaknesses keeping me from Him. Perhaps I will realize my words of unworthiness are only an empty platitude. Yet they could become a reality. Then the contrast between my unworthiness and what my Eucharistic Redeemer calls me could be amazing.

Perhaps I will remember the extraordinary words of Jesus directed to the father who asked for his son to be cured from epilepsy while hardly believing He had that power. Maybe I will remember God's astonishment over his disbelief. God has a liking for men of violence, for these mad ones who conquer the Kingdom of Heaven (cf. Mt. 11:12). They conquer, not being worthy of this Kingdom. God does not call the decent to sanctity but sinners.

Thanks to grace I can realize the power of His word. After all, by the power of His word the greatest miracle of the world happens when He descends onto the altar. Such power can be effective in me and open me to grace before Holy Communion. Repeating the prayer deeply rooted in the centurion's words: "Lord, I am not worthy . . ."—I will be speaking with faith: "only say the word"—this word that has no limits to its power. It can transform my heart and heal my soul **right now**.

Only healing? Maybe. These crazy ones like *"men of violence"* who conquer the kingdom of heaven will turn to Jesus: *Speak . . ., and my soul will be sanctified.* I should not put up barriers to His infinite power and love. After all, it may be that God in the Eucharist, by the power of these marvelous words, will in a certain moment effect my transformation.

You'll effect this when I receive You sometime. When I receive You into my heart, I will be no more. There will be only You, my God and Lord, my only hope. Just You along with Holy Communion will grant me the grace of uniting me with Yourself in love.

This looks like madness, but Jesus coming in the Eucharist crazily loves me and longs to dwell in me. He wishes me to live in union with Him. So I may be with Him for grace and glory, prepared by my Eucharistic Lord.

Defenseless Love

*B*ehold, I stand at your door and knock. . ."
(cf. Rev. 3:20).

Jesus in the Eucharist would like me to knock hard. He wants to provoke my prayer and to be dependent on me, one of little faith.

I am wrapped up in myself. That is how I like it. I am standing at the door leading to Your Eucharistic Heart. It is hard for me to be on the other side. Teach me to knock hard. I still want to try. In fact, I have no hope the door will ever open. Maybe I don't want it to.

It is not so easy to knock. Even though it means being in touch with You, I don't know how to do it. Teach me, hidden Eucharistic One, more and more to expect You and get in touch with You. A child can knock by kicking at the door, but I am no longer a child. I don't knock very hard since I only want a certain amount of You.

Eucharistic Jesus, help me see it is so easy to find myself on the other side of the door leading to Your Heart. If by being small I get needy of You, You are ready to make the first move to open the door wide. You hurry to open it more than I hurry to enter.

Actually, You have already opened it. I keep shutting it. I shut myself behind it, crazily running away. Only Your Eucharistic presence can teach me how to calm down just for a moment, to listen so that eventually I find myself in Your arms, convinced of Your reality.

I want to tell You, Eucharistic Lord, that I can only knock because You allow it. I should admit it is You who are constantly knocking. I am the one who doesn't want to open the door. It is amazing You want to be dependent on me, a sinner. Such is my strange behavior. You are exhausted looking for me, even to the point of the Cross, yet I am so indifferent and distant. You die for me. You come on the altar for me, giving me freedom to accept or reject You.

You have to teach me everything; You have to teach me how to recognize Your defenseless love. I have still not discovered Your true face.

St. Catherine of Siena tells us that if we were really convinced that God loves us more than we love ourselves, our anxieties would simply wither away.

In the Mass, I join in those provocative words in the Our Father. As I pray that most amazing word—*Father*—I am helped to remember what happens in the Mass.

To become a human father is to assume full dependence on a little child who is utterly dependent on father. We get "omnipotent" over the father's heart!

We depend so much on people who depend on us. The strong one is completely defenseless toward the weak. The weak one trusts him so he can't be left. To love this small child means to depend on him or her in an unavoidable way. A child is given enormous power over the father.

With this analogy, I can get a brilliant insight of faith. I can begin to see how God loves me in this demanding fashion. He gives me power over Himself. I am free to respond. He suffered on the

Cross because He loved me and lovingly gave Himself for me.

Faith's insight leads me to recognize the truth that the Eucharistic One is always "weaker" than I. I can disavow and forget Him but He can't forget me. I may cease to be a son. He can't cease to be a Father. Our Eucharistic Lord is always "weaker" than I because His love is ceaseless.

The ones who love become defenseless toward the ones they love. By loving, I open myself to possible injury. I can only be injured by one I love. The more I love, the more I can be injured.

To understand a little of the greatness of this opening to injury in our Eucharistic Lord, we need to note the fantastic quality of His love. In this mysterious Sacrament, the greatest love reveals: ". . . Jesus continues, in the sacrament of the Eucharist, to love us 'to the end,' even to offering us His body and His blood."[26] I will never sufficiently penetrate this love. I long to gaze onto the Eucharistic species, but the enormity of God's defenseless love open to injury remains a mystery.

---

26. Benedict XVI, *Sacramentum Caritatis,* 1.

Yet the Eucharistic Lamb wants to give me eternity to fathom this infinite love. Then I will be at the source of eternal admiration and happiness.

If I start here and now, I will let the Eucharist fully operate within me so that His grace permeates me thoroughly. To some extent I will discover the true face of Jesus, so defenseless and weak. Perhaps I will be rather like St. Paul. He the persecutor discovered that Jesus allowed him to persecute Him because His love is defenseless. He discovered His crazy love. His discovery of the Lord had him forever trying to communicate it.

"For I will show him how much he must suffer for the sake of my name" (Acts 9:16). Yet He also made him an extraordinary pillar of the Church. Paul couldn't imagine what would follow. Neither could He wish it. He had no idea how he would be led to God.

Abraham too had no idea where God would lead him. It turned out to be better than he imagined. During his life he saw Canaan occupied while still a nomad. He was however gradually growing to such great faith that he was called the father of faith. He was maturing in faith when he sacrificed his son in a way many Christians couldn't imitate. His future was unimaginable and unexpected. Such a dedicated one is a father of faith.

If I discover just a little of the Eucharistic Jesus's amazing love for me and wish to respond, it will be in a way I can't imagine or expect. He will finally give me the grace of complete union with Him. It will be granted in an unimaginable and unexpected way with my own consent and desire. When we closely take notice of people greatly dedicated to God, the impact of His grace is visible. Eucharistic graces greatly transformed them. In time of trial we can be greatly disappointed, apostolic efforts can be really unsuccessful on account of intrigue, greed, or meanness.

All these setbacks highlight realities from appearances. Through the rubble and ruins, in the long, silent prayer of faith, it becomes clear that those setbacks were illusory.

Our unfathomable God on the Cross lost everything humanly. Yet the regular renewal of this in the sacrificial Mass, compellingly inspires more and more dedication. New saints appear all the time. It is apparent that all the setbacks, lack of success, and losses were quite unreal.

We can receive light to understand that everything Jesus wants is best. It is only self-will that leads to disaster. We may think we are ruined. It is not worth one tear. It is just illusions.

Finally we can discover that our hidden Eucharistic God wanted the uselessness of our needless activity. He doesn't need our action. He doesn't wait for our results. He needs us just to need Him.

Having nothing makes space for God's grace in acts of pure love. As St. John of the Cross tells us, that means more than all the deeds taken together.[27]

Look, our Eucharistic Lord says, *your pride has failed you. Nobody wants you. You have no peace or happiness. You pray with the words: Lord, I have nothing and have done no good in my life.*

When I pray like this, our Eucharistic Lord answers by conquering souls in His calm usual way: *You are My love and My glory. You think nobody needs you. I make you into a likeness of Me. I look on you with unlimited love. My crazy, amazing love inspires you in the most extraordinary ways.*

---

27. Cf. St. John of the Cross, *The Spiritual Canticle*, 29,2.